100 YEARS OF POPULAR

90s - Volume 1

9 0 s

Series Editor:
Carol Cuellar

Editorial and Production:
Artemis Music Limited

Design and Production:
JPCreativeGroup.com

Published 2003

International Music Publications Limited
Griffin House 161 Hammersmith Road London W6 8BS England

CONTENTS

90s

December 31, 1999. . . How fresh the images that filled our television screens still seem: thick crowds in London's Docklands, the throng at New York's Times Square, revellers dancing on the Champs-Elysees, and awe-struck faces looking up at the fireworks on Sydney's waterfront, as the world greeted the arrival of a new millennium. In the background, the TV presenter was opining about the profound changes that had taken place in the 1900s, a century that began with people travelling by horse-drawn carriages and ended with them living for months at a time in outer space.

Change was indeed the watchword of the 20th Century, and at no time did it take place with more stunning speed than in the 1990s. Earlier advances, like the development of the radio and automobile, moved at a slower pace, evolving over a span of generations. But in the frenetic '90s, new inventions seemed to enter our daily lives as quickly as digital images pop up on a computer monitor.

For example, suppose the worldwide millennium celebration of 1999 had taken place a decade earlier. Very few people in the crowd at the Millennium Dome would have had a cell phone, fewer still would have ever sent an e-mail, and almost none of them would be familiar with terms like "fax machine", "website", or "e-commerce". Yet, all of these features of the Information Age were instantly familiar to the celebrants that welcomed the new millennium, regardless of which corner of our rapidly shrinking world they called home.

The '90s were more than a decade of technological advances. They were an era of transformation, ten years that altered the way we define space and time and interconnected us in ways that few could have imagined on January 1, 1990.

This spirit of change was reflected in the hit songs of the decade. Pop and rock music underwent a profound transformation in the '90s, as alternative sounds that had been fermenting in acid houses, rave clubs, and other underground haunts bubbled up into the mainstream. From the spacious sonically textured sound of ambient music, to the raw power of hip hop, hi-NRG, and techno rave, these new influences energised popular music, setting it aglow with an edgy vitality that both challenged and excited fans who took the time to listen.

New Voices

Young artists like the Scottish duo of Bill Drummond and Jimmy Cauty, who made up the group the KLF (the "Kopyright Liberation Front"), were influential in popularising the electronica sound. Their 1992 single "Justified & Ancient", recorded with American country legend Tammy Wynette, was a hit on both sides of the Atlantic.

Another British group, Blur, which grew out of The Stone Roses, became leaders of the "Brit Pop" sound of the mid '90s. Their provocative and freewheeling single "Beetlebum", which runs through the Fab Four's entire White Album in a five-minute track, was one of the more innovative recordings of the decade.

The '90s also saw the arrival of a new generation of bright and assertive female stars. Inspired by the phenomenal success of Madonna a decade earlier, female artists from American Sheryl Crow to Welsh singer/songwriter Donna Lewis burst on the scene in the '90s with hits like "All I Wanna Do" and "I Love You Always Forever".

Avoiding the often-passive themes of earlier "girl songs", which centred around dealing with boyfriend problems, the music of these female artists took a woman's point of view of life and love. In the '90s, more than in any previous decade, the image of the tough, make-your-own-rules rock star was as likely to be filled by a female as a male artist.

Girl Power extended beyond the assertive rock of Sheryl Crow or the up-tempo adult contemporary sound of Donna Lewis. Female artists also showed that they could be every bit as good as the boys when it came to being teenage idols.

Geri Halliwell, Melanie Brown, Melanie Chisholm, and Victoria Adams, later joined by Emma Bunton, were five former models and actresses who became a pop culture phenomenon in the middle of the decade as The Spice Girls. The group's 1996 release "Wannabe" was the first debut single by an all-female band to reach No.1 on the UK charts. The song held onto the top position for an impressive seven weeks. Before the year was over, it had reached No.1 in 21 nations outside of England.

With their attractive looks, colourful personalities, and charismatic stage presence, The Spice Girls were able to reach out beyond the teen market and appeal to fans of all ages. For many, they came to symbolise a hip new "Cool Britannia" image of the UK that swept Europe and North America in the second half of the '90s, when *Newsweek* magazine described London as the coolest capital on earth.

The '90s also saw the emergence of one of the world's most beloved and commercially successful female stars, Celine Dion. Although the Quebec-born singer has sold over 100 million albums in her spectacular career, she was all but unknown outside of Canada and France in the late '80s, when she and her manager and future husband Rene Angelil embarked on an 18-month plan to remake her image and improve her English. Their efforts paid off handsomely in the new decade, as Dion emerged as a major star in the US and UK, thanks to songs like "Because You Loved Me", a beautiful ballad from the film *Up Close And Personal*.

Urban And Retro Sound

As Dion and Angelil so well understood, the world was rapidly becoming a smaller place as the '80s gave way to the '90s. As befits an era

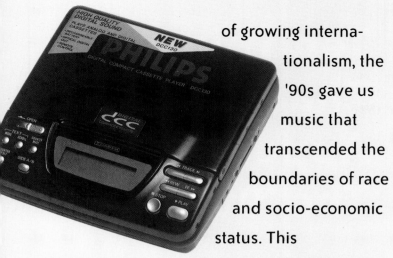

of growing internationalism, the '90s gave us music that transcended the boundaries of race and socio-economic status. This phenomenon is exemplified by the career of British soul artist Seal, whose given name was Sealhenry Samuel.

Born to Nigerian and Brazilian parents and raised in London, Seal emerged from the house music scene to blaze a new path in British soul music in the mid-'90s. A brilliant and adventuresome vocalist, he was able to fuse soul, dance, rock, and folk influences into his distinctive music. Seal's stylish and intimate sound made him a star in Europe and North America. In 1995, his song "Kiss From A Rose" was featured in the film *Batman Forever*. This sent the song soaring up the charts, helping its album *Seal* achieve multi-platinum status.

Lisa Stansfield from Manchester was another great '90s artist who forged a dynamic new urban sound that appealed to fans from all walks of life. The Brit Award and Ivor Novello Award-winning artist reached a broad audience in the UK and other countries with her passionate and reflective brand of soul, jazz, and dance music. Stansfield's lush emotive ballad "All Woman", about a long-suffering wife, was a Top 20 hit in the UK.

Although the '90s was a decade of new sounds and new stars, it was also a time when tried-and-true music genres reappeared with new life as part of a "retro trend". The 1993 hit "Are You Gonna Go My Way" from American artist Lenny Kravitz was one of the more important retro songs of the early decade. With its blistering guitar work and rollicking sound, the song evoked strong images of rock's hard-driving roots, powering it to the Top Five on the UK charts.

The American artist Marvin Lee Aday, better known as Meatloaf, who had been one of the pre-eminent hard rockers of the 1970s and early '80s, saw his career revived during the retro wave of the '90s. His 1993 album *Bat Out Of Hell II, Back Into Hell* sold over 10 million copies and spawned the No.1 UK and US hit "I'd Do Anything For Love, (But I Won't Do That)".

In the same year that Kravitz and Meatloaf were tearing up the charts, British guitar legend Brian May of Queen was reaching the UK Top 10 with the solo hit "Driven By You". This electrifying song was featured in a Ford car commercial in Britain, earning May a 1993 Ivor Novello Award.

May's group Queen saw its glorious career

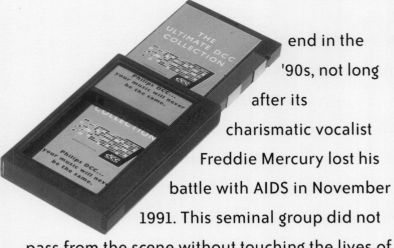

end in the '90s, not long after its charismatic vocalist Freddie Mercury lost his battle with AIDS in November 1991. This seminal group did not pass from the scene without touching the lives of countless fans. Its album *Innuendo*, which was recorded after Mercury was diagnosed with AIDS, debuted at No.1 on the UK charts. Among the album's hits was the reflective "These Are The Days Of Our Lives", a song made more poignant and meaningful in light of Mercury's illness.

In April 1992, the surviving members of Queen, along with an all-star ensemble of rock stars, held a memorial concert for Freddie Mercury at Wembley Stadium. An estimated one billion people around the world viewed the concert on television. Although the decade was still young at the time of this concert, the performance at Wembley seemed to capture the spirit of the '90s, a time when, thanks to the power of new technology, great music could speak to people everywhere.

Ten Things That First Appeared In The '90s

1. *Toy Story*, the first full-length feature film to be totally digital.

2. Dolly the Sheep, the first cloned mammal.

3. Pokemon cards.

4. Wonder bra.

5. Viagra.

6. The National Lottery.

7. Sony Play Station.

8. Laser pens.

9. Tamagotchi virtual pets.

10. Stack trainers shoes.

ARE YOU GONNA GO MY WAY?

Words and Music by LENNY KRAVITZ and CRAIG ROSS

Are you gonna go my way?

'Cos ba-by I got to know.

VERSE 2:
I don't know why we always cry,
This we must leave and get undone.
We must engage and rearrange
And turn this planet back to one.
So tell me why we got to die
And kill each other one by one.
We've got to hug and rub-a-dub,
We've got to dance and be in love.
But what I really want to know is
Are you gonna go my way?
And I got to, got to know.

ALL I WANNA DO

Words and Music by SHERYL CROW, WILLIAM BOTTRELL, KEVIN GILBERT
WYN COOPER and DAVID BAERWALD

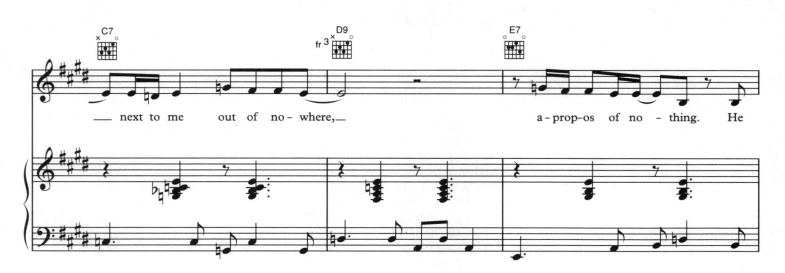

says his name is Wil-liam, but I'm sure he's Bill or Bil-ly or Mac or Bud-dy. But he's

plain ug-ly to me and I won-der if he's ev-er had___ a day of fun in his___whole life.
(see additional lyrics)

— We are drink-ing beer at noon on Tues-day in a bar___that fac - es a gi- ant

car-wash. And the good peo-ple of the world are wash - ing their cars on their lunch break,

San - ta Mo - ni - ca Bou - le - vard.

O - ther- wise the bar is ours, and the day and the night and the

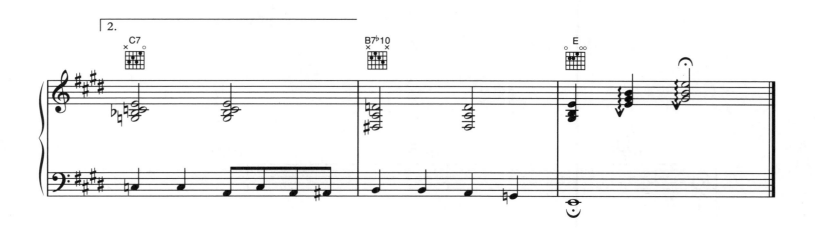

Verse 3:
I like a good beer buzz early in the morning
And Billy likes to peel the labels from his bottles of Bud
And shred them on the bar
Then he lights every match in an oversized pack
Letting each one burn down to his thick fingers
Before blowing and cursing them out
And he's watching the Buds as they spin on the floor
A happy couple enters the bar, dancing dangerously close to one another
The bartender looks up from his want ads

ALL WOMAN

Words and Music by STANSFIELD, DEVANEY and MORRIS

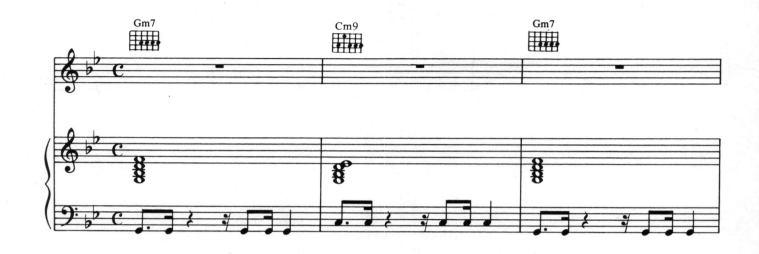

(1.) He's home a-gain_ from an-oth-er day, she
(Verses 2 & 3, see at bottom)

smiles at him as he walks through the door._ She won-ders if it will

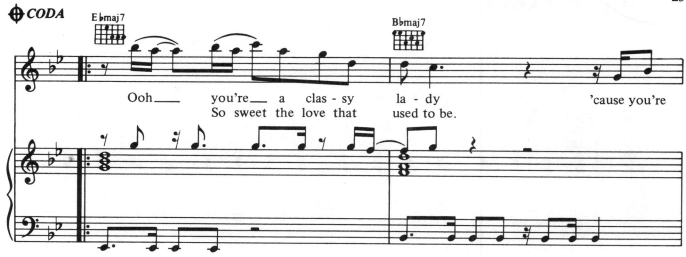

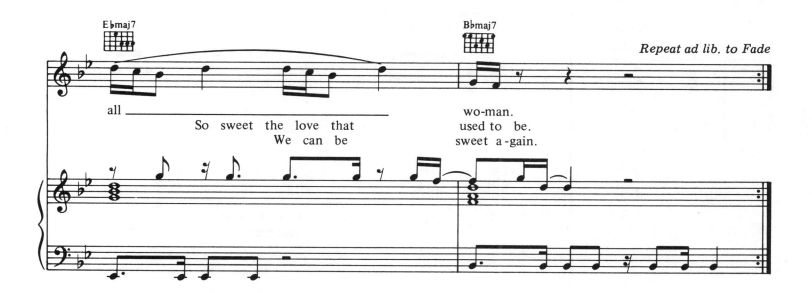

VERSE 2:

She stands there and lets the tears flow
Tears that she's been holding back so long
She wonders where did all the loving go
The love they used to share when they were strong.

She says yes, I look a mess
But I don't love you any less
I thought you always thought enough of me
To always be impressed.

CHORUS 2:

I may not be a lady
But I'm all woman
From Monday to Sunday I work my fingers to the bone
I'm no classy lady
But I'm all woman
This woman needs a little love to make her strong
You're not the only one.

VERSE 3:

He holds her and hangs his head in shame
He doesn't see her like he used to do
He's too wrapped up in working for his pay
He hasn't seen the pain he's put her through.

Attention that he paid
Just vanished in the haze
He remembers how it used to be
When he used to say.

CHORUS 3:

You'll always be a lady
'Cause you're all woman
From Monday to Sunday I love you much more than you know
You're a classy lady
'Cause you're all woman
This woman needs a loving man to keep her warm.

BACK FOR GOOD

Words and Music by GARY BARLOW

BE MY BABY

Words by LENNY KRAVITZ and GERRY DEVEAUZ
Music by LENNY KRAVITZ

I want you to love___ me ba - by.

Repeat to Fade

VERSE 2:
Love is just like a flower, baby it has to grow, yeah.
And when you are away I'm even loving you more.
I just have to let you know
One on one is the way and that's the way it should be, yeah.
So if you're not gonna stay then don't be playing with me,
You can set me free.

CHORUS 2:
All I'm asking you for when you walk out the door
Is to be my baby, baby
'Cause all this love is for you and you know that I'm true
And I'll be your baby.
Continue to additional chorus

(D.S.) VERSE 3:
I remember our walk the other Saturday night,
Sweet harmonies filled and floated through our minds.
Never felt this way before.
We were riding so high on love and understanding,
So why go wasting your time when you have got such a find
That is everlasting?

CHORUS 3: — As Chorus 1⁰

ADDITIONAL CHORUS:
All I'm asking you for when you walk out the door
Is to be my baby, baby
'Cause all this love is for you and you know that I'm true,
And I'll be your baby.
To Coda

BECAUSE YOU LOVED ME

Words and Music by DIANE WARREN

love I found in you,___ I'll be for-ev-er thank-ful, ba-by.
love, I had___ it all.___ I'm grate-ful for each day___ you gave___ me.

You're the one___ who held___ me up, ne-ver let___ me fall.___
May-be I___ don't know___ that much, but I know this much is true.___

You're the one___ who saw___ me through, through it all.___
I was blessed be-cause___ I was loved by you.___ You were___ my

strength when I___ was weak, you were my voice when I could-n't speak. You were my

BREAKFAST AT TIFFANY'S

Words and Music by TOBY PIPES

Moderately

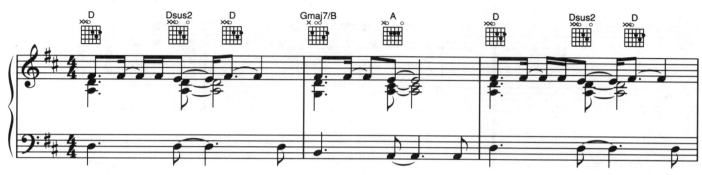

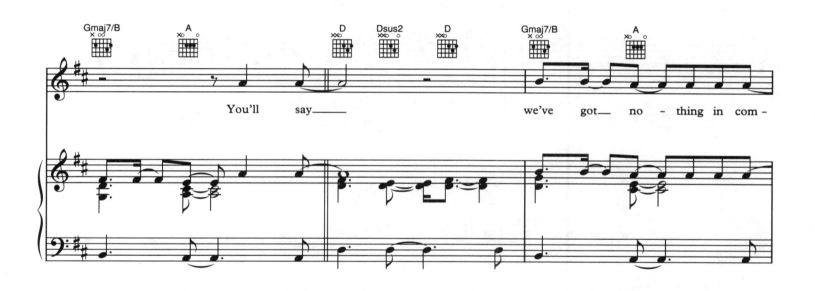

You'll say____ we've got__ no - thing in com-

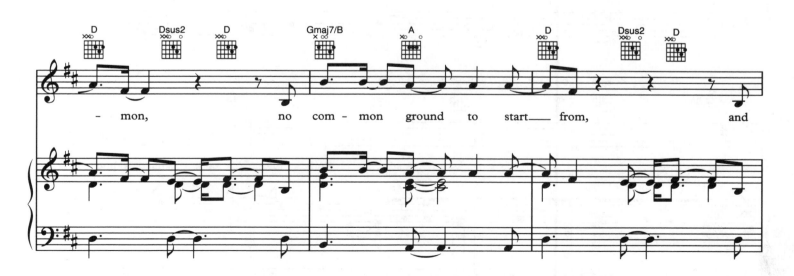

- mon, no com - mon ground to start____ from, and

BEETLEBUM

Words and Music by DAMON ALBARN, STEVEN ALEXANDER JAMES,
GRAHAM COXON and DAVID ROWNTREE

He's on, he's on, he's on___ it. He's on, he's on, he's on___ it.___

He's on, he's on, he's on___ it. He's on, he's on, he's on___ it.

repeat and fade

CLEMENTINE

Words and Music by MARK OWEN

Moderately

She heard a voice from so far a-way, it told her her mo-ther had
Got in her car and she sped a-way in-to the flood-lit street, down

gone a-way.__ In the next room down the cor-ri-dor her
by your__ way. As the sun rose through the morn-ing dew, well, she re-

ba – by start-ed to cry.__ Her whole life had just fell
-turned__ in such a__ state.__ Her ba – by knew not what was

CRAZY

Words and Music by SEALHENRI SAMUEL and GUY SIGSWORTH

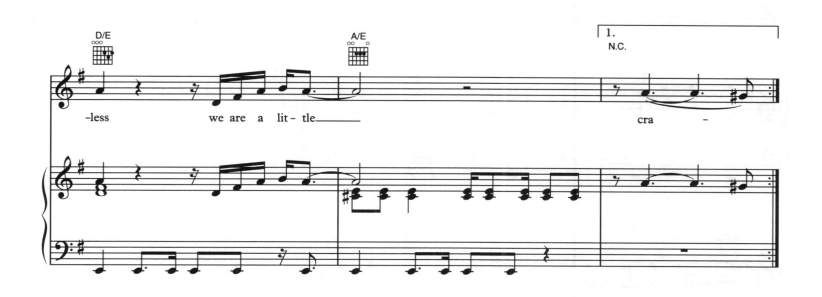

-less   we are a lit - tle____   cra -

Oh   no,___ we'll ne - ver sur - vive_____   un - less we get a lit - tle____

___ bit._____

D.% *repeat and fade*

cra - zy.

Verse 2:

Yellow people walking through my head
One of them's got a gun to shoot the other one
And yet together they were friends at school
(Yeah, yeah, yeah)
If I were there when we first took the pill
Then maybe . . .
Miracles will happen as we speak

DAMN, I WISH I WAS YOUR LOVER

Words and Music by SOPHIE B HAWKINS

DON'T LET GO (LOVE)

Words and Music by IVAN MATIAS, ANDREA MARTIN,
MARQUEZE ETHERIDGE and ORGANIZED NOIZE

DON'T LET THE SUN GO DOWN ON ME

Words and Music by ELTON JOHN and BERNIE TAUPIN

THE DRUGS DON'T WORK

Words and Music by RICHARD ASHCROFT

(1.)___ you're think - ing of___ me   as you lay down   on___ your   side.
(2.)___ I'm on___ a los - ing streak   as I pass down   my___ old   street.
(3.)___ of get - ting old,_____   it's get - ting me   down___ my   love.

Now the drugs don't work,___ they just make you___ worse___ but I___ know I'll see your face
And if you want a show   just let me___ know___ and I'll___ sing in your ear___
Like a cat in a bag   wait - ing to drown___   this time I'm com -

___ a - gain._
___ a - gain._
- ing down.

Now the drugs don't work,___ they just make you___ worse

___ but I___ know I'll see your face___ a - gain.

2. But I know___

Coz ba - by ooh,_____ if hea - ven calls_

I'm com - ing too.___ Just like you say,_____

you'll leave my life,___ I'm bet - ter off dead.___ 3. All this talk_

to Coda ⊕ *D.% al Coda*

END OF THE ROAD

Words and Music by BABYFACE, L A REID and DARYL SIMMONS

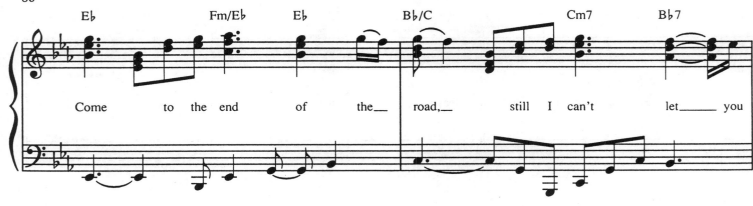

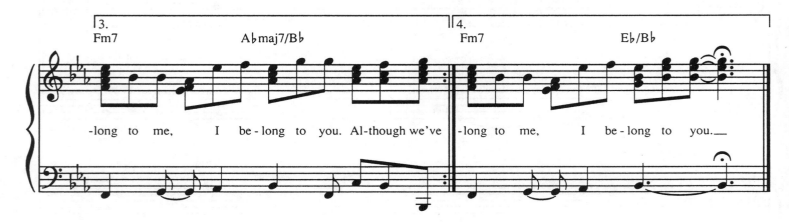

Verse 2:
Girl, I know you really love me, you just don't realize.
You've never been there before, it's only your first time.
Maybe I'll forgive you, mmm. . . maybe you'll try.
We should be happy together, forever, you and I.

Bridge 2:
Could you love me again like you loved me before?
This time, I want you to love me much more.
This time, instead just come back to my bed.
And baby, just don't let me down.

Verse 3, spoken:
Girl I'm here for you.
All those times at night when you just hurt me,
And just ran out with that other fellow,
Baby, I knew about it.
I just didn't care.
You just don't understand how much I love you, do you?
I'm here for you.
I'm not out to go out there and cheat all night just like you did, baby.
But that's alright, huh, I love you anyway.
And I'm still gonna be here for you 'til my dyin' day, baby.
Right now, I'm just in so much pain, baby,
'Cause you just won't come back to me, will you?
Just come back to me.

Bridge 3, spoken:
Yes, baby, my heart is lonely.
My heart hurts, baby, yes, I feel pain too.
Baby please . . .

FLY AWAY

Words and Music by LENNY KRAVITZ

*R.H. tacet 1st time (next 8 bars only). Omit notes in parentheses 2nd time.

I wish that I could fly into the sky so ver-y high,
Let's go and see the stars, the Milk-y Way or e-ven Mars,

just like a drag-on-fly.
where it could just be ours.

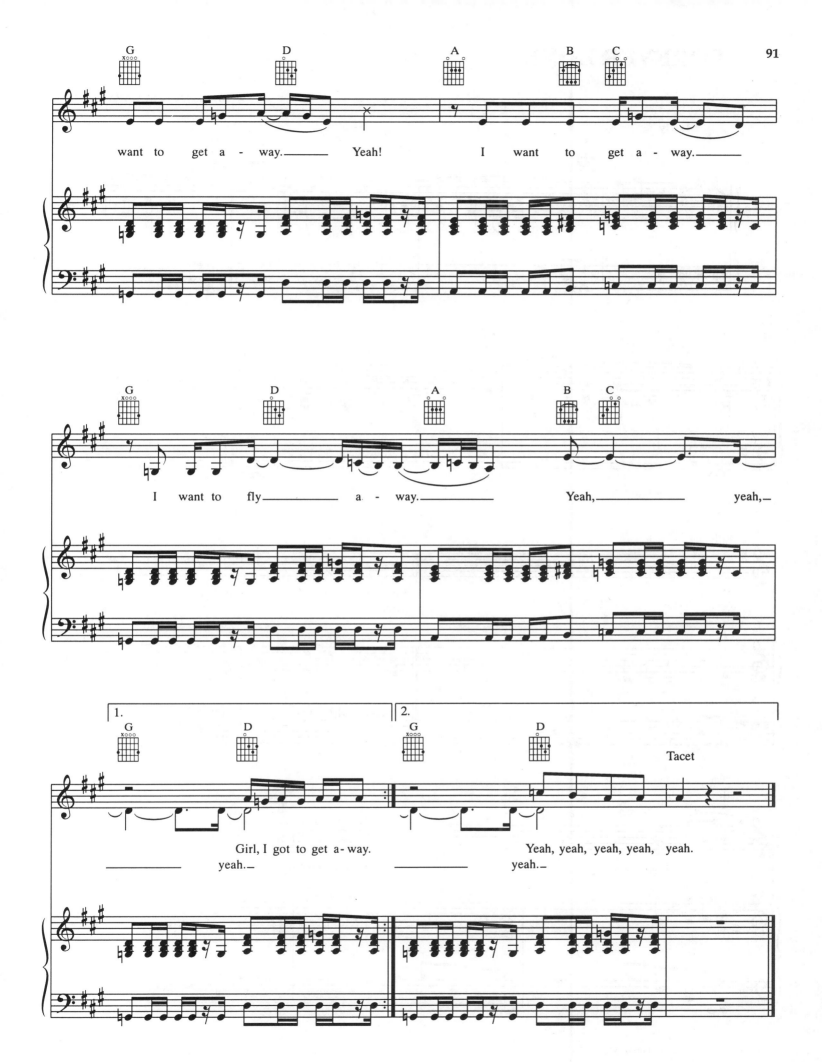

FOREVER LOVE

Words and Music by GARY BARLOW

Slowly

Love it has__ so ma-ny beau-ti-ful fa-
(Instrumental)

-ces,

shar-ing lives____

FROM A DISTANCE

Words and Music by JULIE GOLD

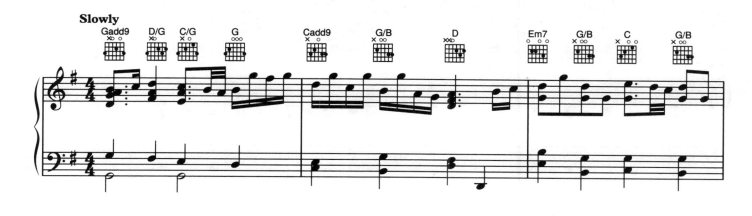

From a dis-tance, the world looks blue___ and green,___ and the
(see additional lyrics)

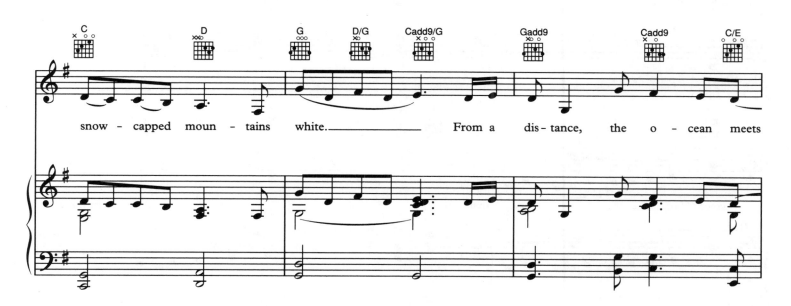

snow-capped moun-tains white._____ From a dis-tance, the o-cean meets

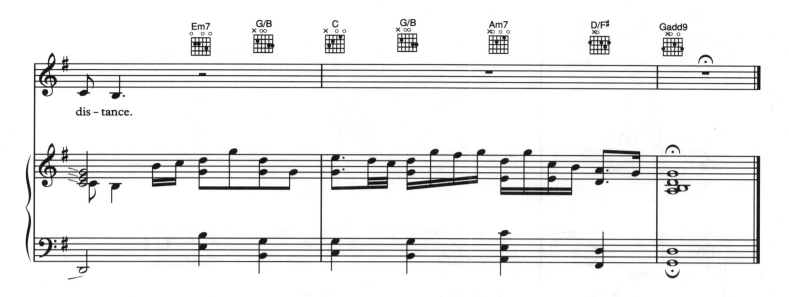

dis – tance.

Verse 2:
From a distance, we all have enough
And no one is in need
There are no guns, no bombs, no diseases
No hungry mouths to feed
From a distance, we are instruments
Marching in a common band
Playing songs of hope, playing songs of peace
They're the songs of every man

Verse 3:
From a distance, you look like my friend
Even though we are at war
From a distance I just cannot comprehend
What all this fighting is for
From a distance there is harmony
And it echoes through the land
It's the hope of hopes, it's the love of loves
It's the heart of every man

GET HERE

Words and Music by BRENDA RUSSELL

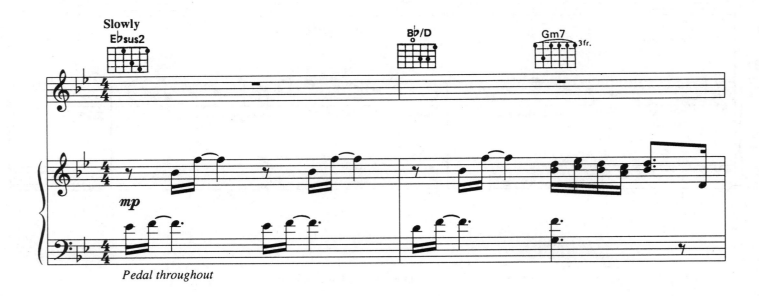

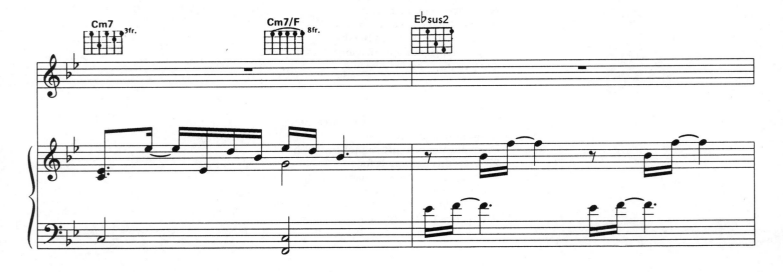

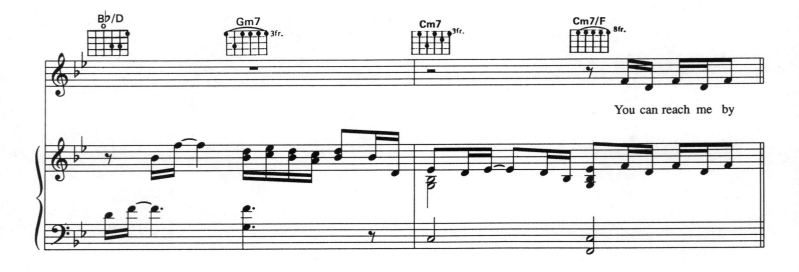

You can reach me by

GOING OUT

Words and Music by DANIEL GOFFEY, GARETH COOMBES
MICHAEL QUINN and ROBERT COOMBES

Moderately

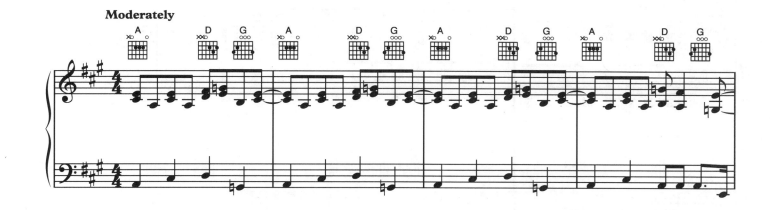

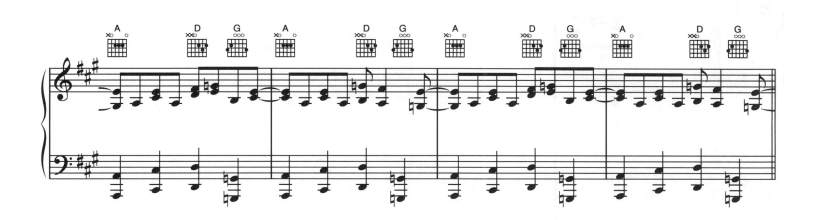

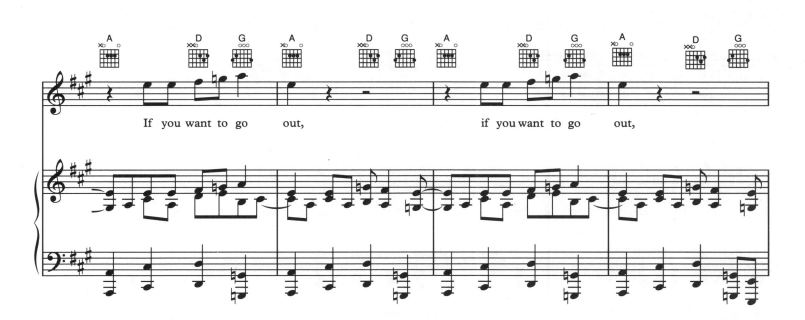

If you want to go out, if you want to go out,

oh no.

oh no.

HEAL THE WORLD

Written and Composed by MICHAEL JACKSON
Prelude by MARTY PAICH

I WILL ALWAYS LOVE YOU

Words and Music by DOLLY PARTON

Verse 3: Instrumental solo

Verse 4:
I hope life treats you kind
And I hope you have all you've dreamed of.
And I wish to you, joy and happiness.
But above all this, I wish you love.
(To Chorus:)

I LOVE YOU ALWAYS FOREVER

Words and Music by DONNA LEWIS

ev-ery-thing, I___ will do for you. I love you, al-ways for-ev-er, near and far, clos-er to-ge-ther.

repeat ad lib. and fade

Ev-ery-where, I___ will be with you, ev-ery-thing, I___ will do for you.

Verse 3:
You've got the most unbelievable blue eyes I've ever seen
You've got me almost melting away as we lay there
Under blue sky with pure white stars
Exotic sweetness, a magical time

I WANNA BE THE ONLY ONE

Words and Music by RHETT LAWRENCE and BEBE WINANS

I'D DO ANYTHING FOR LOVE (BUT I WON'T DO THAT)

Words and Music by JIM STEINMAN

No, I won't do ___ that.

Some days it don't ___ come eas - y,
Some nights you're breath - ing fire,
Some days I pray ___ for si - lence,

some days it don't ___ come hard. ___
some nights you're carved ___ in ice. ___
some days I pray ___ for soul. ___

IT'S MY LIFE

Words and Music by DR ALBAN and DENNIZ POP

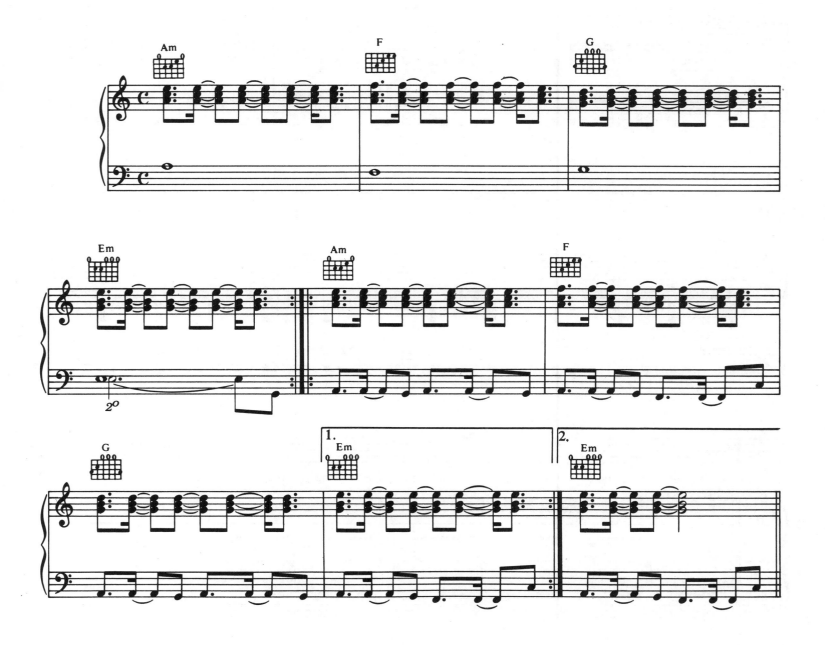

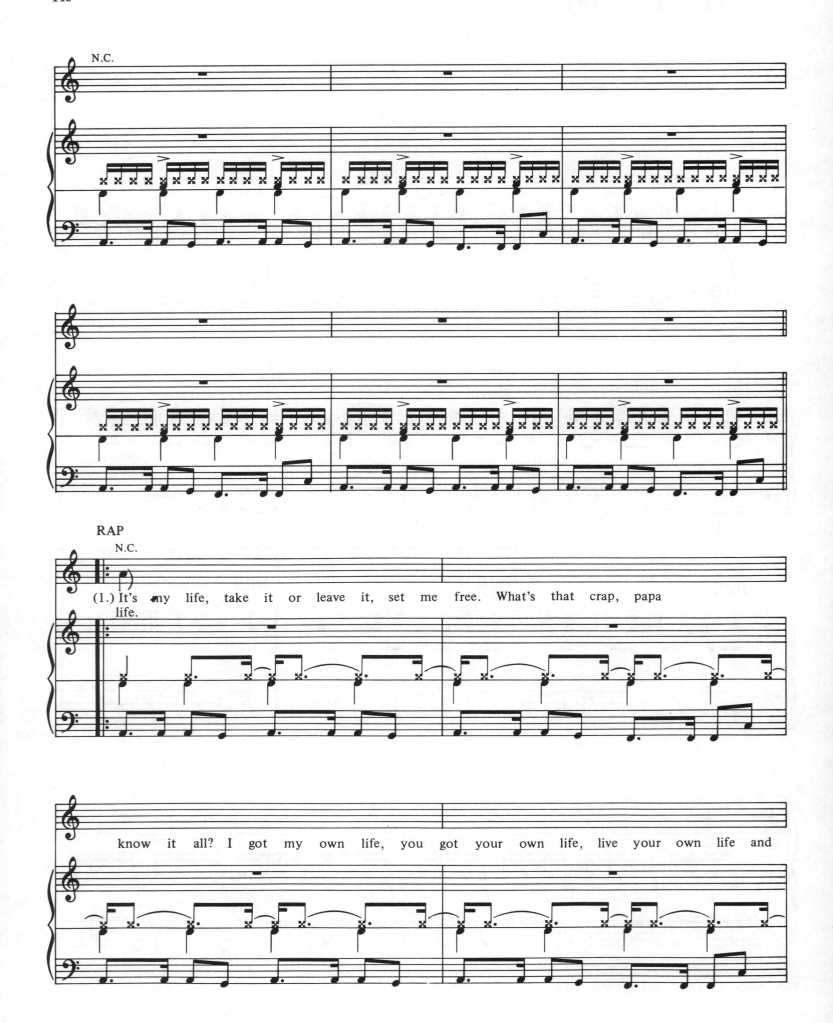

RAP

(1.) It's my life, take it or leave it, set me free. What's that crap, papa
life.

know it all? I got my own life, you got your own life, live your own life and

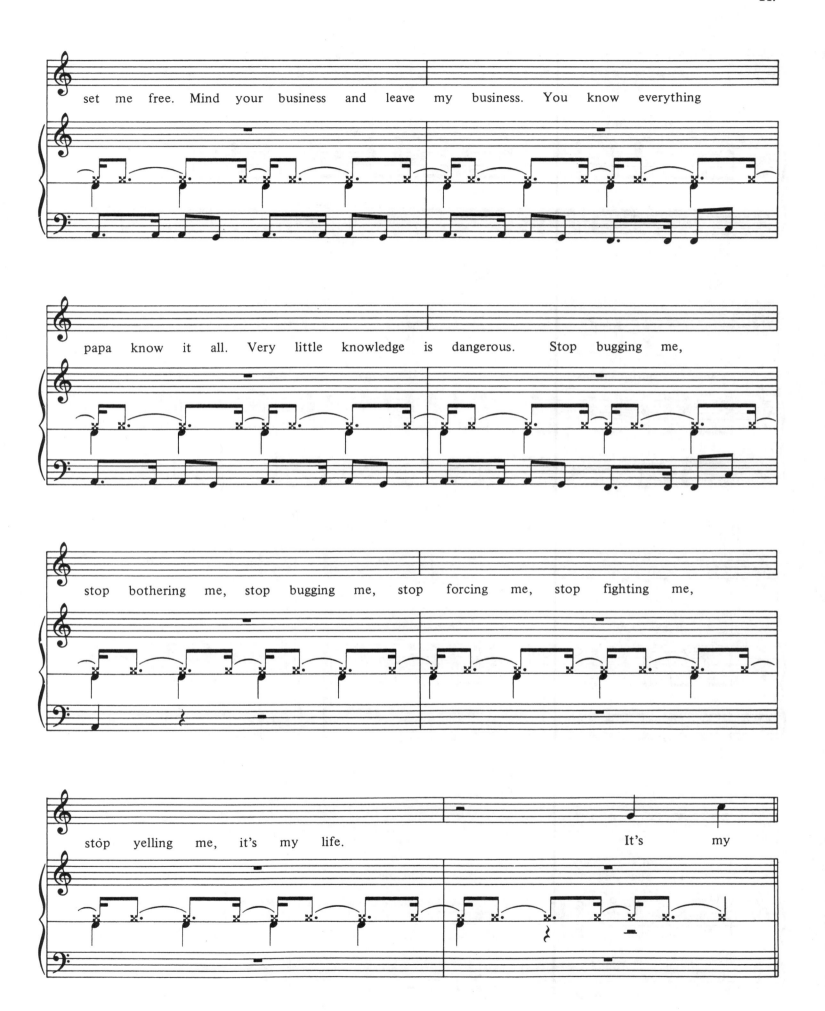

RAP 2:
Do you understand? I live the way I want to live,
I make decisions day and night, show me signs and good examples.
Stop telling people how to run your business, take a trip to East and West.
You find that you don't know anything, every's getting tired of you.
Sometimes you have to look and listen, you can even learn from me.
Little knowledge is dangerous, it's my life.

RAP 3:
Set me free, so you bad so you lie
What you see is what you get, listen to people and sort things out.
Things I do I do them no more, things I say I say them no more.
Changes comes once in life; stop hugging me, stop bothering me,
Stop bugging me, stop forcing me, stop fighting me, stop yelling me,
Stop telling me, stop seeing me, it's my life.

I'LL BE THERE

Words and Music by BERRY GORDY, HAL DAVIES,
WILLIE HUTCH and BOB WEST

2. I'll reach out my hand to you:
   I'll have faith in all you do.
   Just call my name and I'll be there.

3. Let me fill your heart with joy and laughter.
   Togetherness, girl, is all I'm after:
   Whenever you need me, I'll be there.
   I'll be there to protect'you,
   With unselfish love that respects you.
   Just call my name, I'll be there.

JESUS TO A CHILD

Words and Music by GEORGE MICHÆL

153

JUST ANOTHER DAY

Words and Music by JON SECADA and MIGUEL A MOREJON

Verse 2:
Making the time,
Find the right lines to make you stay forever.
What do I have to tell you?
Just trying to hold on to something.
    (Trying to hold on to something good.)
Give us a chance to make it.
    (Give us a chance to make it.)

Bridge 2:
Don't wanna hold on to never . . .
I'm not that strong, I'm not that strong.
(To Chorus:)

Bridge 3:
Why can't you stay forever?
Just give me a reason, give me a reason.
(To Chorus:)

LOVE AIN'T HERE ANYMORE

Words and Music by GARY BARLOW

KISS FROM A ROSE

Words and Music by SAMUEL SEALHENRI

Very slow 2

Capo 3

Ba ya ya ba da ba da da da ba ya ya. Ba ya

ya ba da ba da da da ba ya ya. Ba ya da ba ya ya.

There___ used to be a grey-ing to-wer a-lone on the

sea. You___ be-came the light on the darkside of me.__ But love___ re-mains a

LOVE SHACK

Words and Music by CATHERINE PIERSON, FRED SCHNEIDER
KEITH STRICKLAND and CYNTHIAL WILSON

Love Shack, ba - by.___ Love Shack ba - by.

Love Shack, ba - by, Love___ Shack. Love Shack, ba - by, Love___ Shack.

to Coda ⊕

Love Shack, ba - by, Love___ Shack. Love Shack, ba - by, Love___ Shack.

Sign says, 'Stay a - way, fools,___ 'cause love rules at the
Hug - ging and a kiss - ing, danc - ing and a lov - ing, wear - ing next to no - thing 'cause it's

NORTH COUNTRY BOY

Words and Music by TIMOTHY BURGESS, MARTIN BLUNT, ROBERT COLLINS
JON BROOKES and MARK COLLINS

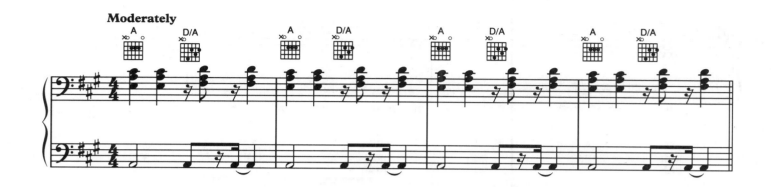

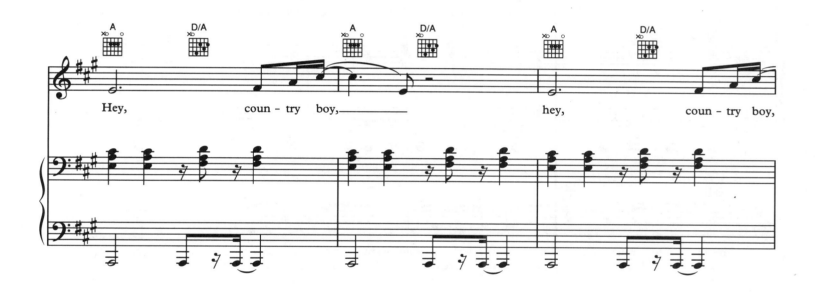

Hey, coun-try boy,_____ hey, coun-try boy,

—— what are you sad a-bout?__ Ev-ery day you make the sun come out,__ ev-en in the

A MILLION LOVE SONGS

Words and Music by GARY BARLOW

mil - lion words just try - ing to make the love song of the year.___

Close your eyes but don't for - get___ what you have heard,___ a

man who's trying to say three words, words that make me scared.___ A mil - lion

love songs___ la - ter___ here I___ am try - ing to tell you___ that I

VERSE 2:
Looking to the future now, this is what I see,
A million chances pass me by, a million chances to hold you.
Take me back, take me back to where I used to be,
Hide away from all my truths, through the light I see.

CHORUS:
A million love songs later,
Here I am trying to tell you that I care.
A million love songs later,
And here I am, just for you girl;
A million love songs later,
Here I am.

MMMBOP

Words and Music by ISAAC HANSON, TAYLOR HANSON
and ZAC HANSON

191

NOVEMBER RAIN

Words and Music by W AXL ROSE, SLASH,
DUFF McKAGAN and IZZY STRADLIN'

Moderately slow

* Recorded a half step lower

201

OLDER

Words and Music by GEORGE MICHAEL

THE ONE AND ONLY

Words and Music by NIK KERSHAW

I am the one and on-ly.

(1.) Call me, call me by my name or
(2.) I've been a play-er in the crowd scene a

PERFECT DAY

Words and Music by LOU REED

You're going to reap___ just what you sow.

play 4 times

Repeat to finish

PEACHES

Words and Music by CHRIS BALLEW, DAVE DEDERER
and JASON FINN

RHYTHM IS A DANCER

Words and Music by BENITO BENITES,
JOHN GARRETT III and THEA AUSTIN

(2nd time cues)

La la la la la la la la

la la la la la la. Ooh.

oh, it's a pas - sion, oh oh oh

oh oh. Rhy-thm, you can feel it, you can feel it,

rhy-thm, rhy-thm is a dan - cer. Rhy-thm,

you can feel it, you can feel it, rhy-thm, rhy-thm is a dan - cer.

RAP:

Let the rhythm ride you, guide you,   sneak inside you, set your mind to move to its pulsation.
When, let it control you   hold you. mould you, not the old,   the new, touch it taste it

Bass vibration, synth sensation   pause, it's not in place   In mind and body must be free to
Free your soul when let it base you   Got to be what you wanna   if the groove don't get you the rhyme flow's

D.%. al Coda

please.   Take it all in,   Nothing to lose everything to...
gonna. I'm serious as cancer when I say   rhythm is a dancer.

CODA

Rhy-thm,   you can feel it, you can feel it,   rhy-thm,

Rhythm to Fade

rhy-thm is   a   dan - cer.

SALTWATER

Words and Music by JULIAN LENNON, LESLIE SPIRO and MARK SPIRO

Verse 2:.
We climb the highest mountain
we'll make the desert bloom
We're so ingenious
We can walk on the moon
But when I hear of how
The forests have died
Saltwater wells in my eyes.

Verse 3:
We light the desert ocean
Send photographs of Mars
We're so enchanted by
How clever we are
Why should one baby
Feel so hungry she cries
Saltwater wells in my eyes.

Verse 4:
We are a rock revolving
Around a golden sun
We are a billion children
Rolled into one
What will I think of me
The day that I die
Saltwater wells in my eyes.

SACRIFICE

Words and Music by ELTON JOHN and BERNIE TAUPIN

cold cold heart

D.%al Coda

CODA

no sa - cri - fice___ at all___

7 SECONDS

Words and Music by CAMERON McVEY, NENEH CHERRY, JONATHAN DOLLAR
and YOUSSOU N'DOUR

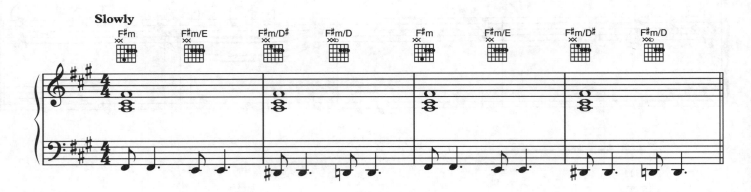

Bul ma seen bul ma djiss ma di re nga fook ni mann xa-mu-ma li nee ka thi

sa ma suul ak thi gui naw Ba-gu-ma ku ma xool daal di ne yaaw Li nee-ka thi yaaw mo

sec - ond. Sev - en sec - onds a - way.___ Just as long as I stay,___ I'll be wait

- ing. It's not a sec - ond. Sev - en sec - onds a - way. Just as long as I

stay,___ I'll be wait - ing. It's not a

SLEEPING SATELLITE

Words and Music by TASMIN ARCHER,
JOHN BECK and JOHN HUGHES

CHORUS

I blame you__ for the moon-lit sky__ and the dream that died__ with the Ea-gles' flight.__ I blame you__ for the moon-lit nights__ when I won-der why__ are the seas still dry?__

VERSE 2:
Have we got what it takes to advance?
Have we peaked too soon?
If the world is so green
Then why does it scream under a blue moon?
We wonder why
If the earth's sacrificed
For the price of its greatest treasure.

VERSE 3 (D.S.)
And when we shoot for the stars
What a giant step;
Have we got what it takes
To carry the weight of this concept
Or pass it by?
Like a shot in the dark
Miss the mark with a sense of adventure.

THE SHOOP SHOOP SONG (IT'S IN HIS KISS)

Words and Music by RUDY CLARK

SHY GUY

Words and Music by DIANA KING, KINGSLEY GARDNER
ANDY MARVEL, HAMISH STUART, STEVE FERRONE
ALAN GORY, ROGER BALL, MALCOLM DUNCAN
and OWEN McINTYRE

SMELLS LIKE TEEN SPIRIT

Words and Music by KURT COBAIN,
CHRIS NOVOSELIC and DAVID GROHL

Load up___ on   guns,___   bring___ your friends.
I'm worse___ at   what___   I ___ do best ___
And I ___ for - get ___ just why ___ I taste. ___

SOMEDAY (I'M COMING BACK)

Words and Music by STANSFIELD, DEVANEY and MORRIS

Some - day I'm com - ing back____ and it won't__ be long__

__ be -fore I'm home,___ home and in___ your arms.__

To Coda ◆

Dno3   Cmaj7

home and in ___ your arms. ___

Em

Some day, ___ some way ___

Am7   Dno3

(I ne - ver want - ed a - ny - thing so ___ much ___
some day, ___

Cmaj7

D.S. (Take repeat back to Chorus, then al Coda)

some way. ___

VERSE 2:
Even in stormy weather, we always stuck together.
You always kept me near, were so sincere.
So why so sudden the change of heart
Why do I feel like I've done wrong?
When all that I want is that you ask me to come back home.

VERSE 3:
(8 bars instrumental)
So why so sudden the change of heart
Why do I feel like I've done wrong?
When all that I want is that you ask me to come back home.

SOMETHING ABOUT THE WAY
YOU LOOK TONIGHT

Words and Music by ELTON JOHN and BERNIE TAUPIN

THESE ARE THE DAYS OF OUR LIVES

Words and Music by QUEEN

Those were____ the days____ of____ our lives,____ yeah,____ the

TOO MUCH LOVE WILL KILL YOU

Words and Music by BRIAN MAY,
FRANK MUSKER and ELIZABETH LAMERS

TO BE WITH YOU

Words and Music by ERIC MARTIN and DAVID GRAHAME

UN-BREAK MY HEART

Words and Music by DIANE WARREN

WANNABE

Words and Music by MATTHEW ROWBOTTOM, RICHARD STANNARD
MELANIE BROWN, VICTORIA AADAMS, GERI HALLIWELL
EMMA BUNTON and MELANIE CHISHOLM

Moderately

VIRTUAL INSANITY

Words by JASON KAY
Music by JASON KAY, TOBY SMITH,
STUART ZENDER, WALLIS BUCHANAN,
DEREK McKENZIE and SIMON KATZ

VOGUE

Words and Music by MADONNA CICCONE and SHEP PETTIBONE

WHAT DO YOU WANT FROM ME?

Words and Music by DAVID POTTS and PETER HOOK

la la la la.___ Sha la la___ la la la la.___

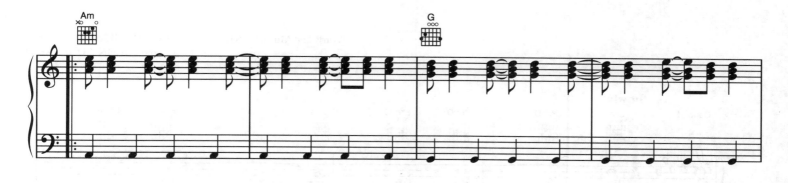

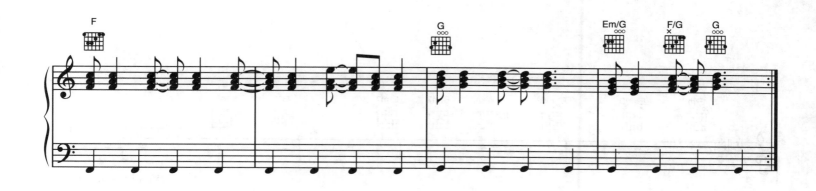

WOMAN

Words and Music by NENEH CHERRY, CAMERON McVEY
and JOHNNY DOLLAR

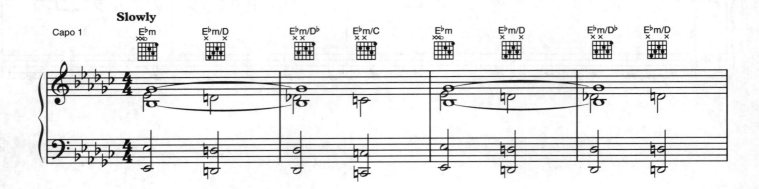

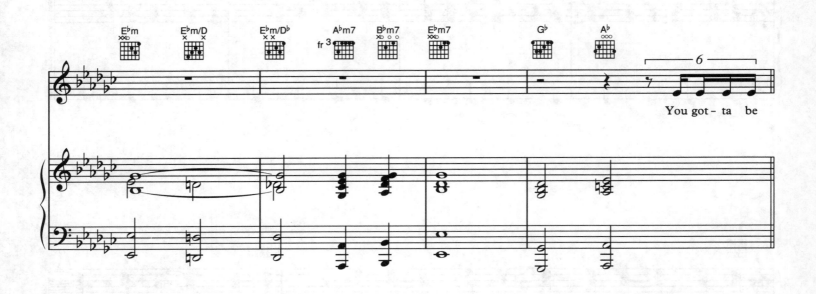

You got-ta be

for-tun-ate, you got-ta be luc-ky now. I was just

WOMAN TO WOMAN

Words and Music by BEVERLEY CRAVEN

Moderate, strong beat

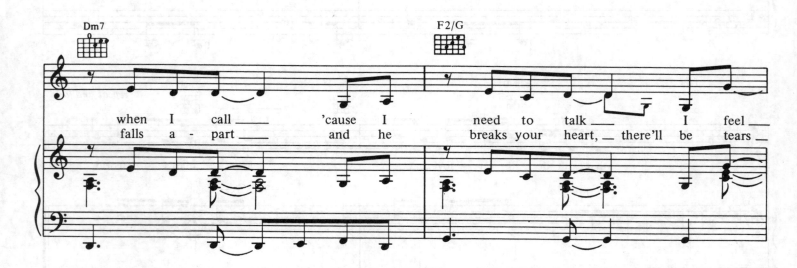

100 YEARS OF POPULAR MUSIC

9816A

Vol. 1 - 9817A

Vol. 2 - 9818A

Vol. 1 - 9819A

Vol. 2 - 9820A

International Music
Publications Limited

Vol. 1 - 9821A

Vol. 2 - 9822A

Vol. 1 - 9823A

Vol. 2 - 9824A

Vol. 1 - 9825A

Vol. 2 - 9826A

Vol. 1 - 9827A

Vol. 2 - 9828A

Vol. 1 - 9829A

Vol. 2 - 9830A

Vol. 1 - 9831A

Vol. 2 - 9832A

9833A

IMP
International
MUSIC
Publications

IMP's Exciting New Series!